FAIR DINKUM!

INTRODUCTION AND COMMENTARY BY

H.G. NELSON

AUSSIE
SLANG

FAIR
DINKUM!

NLA PUBLISHING

NATIONAL
LIBRARY
OF AUSTRALIA

Published by the National Library of Australia
Canberra ACT 2600

© National Library of Australia 2018
First published 2015. Reprinted 2016, 2017 and 2018
Introduction and commentary text © Greig Pickhaver

Books published by the National Library of Australia further the Library's objectives to interpret and highlight the Library's collections and to support the creative work of the nation's writers and researchers.

National Library of Australia Cataloguing-in-Publication entry

Creator: Nelson, H. G., author.
Title: Fair dinkum! : Aussie slang / H.G. Nelson with the National Library of Australia.
ISBN: 9780642278791 (paperback)
Subjects: Australianisms.
                    English language--Australia--Humor.
                    English language--Slang.
Other Creators/
Contributors: National Library of Australia issuing body.
Dewey Number: 427.994

Commissioning publisher: Susan Hall
Editor: Amelia Hartney
Designer: Louise Dews
Image coordinator: Jemma Posch
Production coordinator: Melissa Bush
Printed in China through Asia Pacific Offset

Find out more about National Library Publishing at http://publishing.nla.gov.au.

Front cover image: Anan Kaewkhammul
                    Close up of Australian Emu Head Isolated
                    Shutterstock #196046570
                    www.shutterstock.com

G'DAY!

Language is a powerful weapon and its explosive propellant is slang. As this excellent collection of slang words and phrases demonstrates, Australians have left a unique yellow and green mark on the rich history of the English language.

Our top-of-the-table position at international forums has been all the more notable for our outstanding linguistic contributions: 'Look out world,' we bellowed in late 2014, 'Team Australia is on the burst coming through with a shirtfront!' This demonstrated that the lucky country can still punch above its weight when push comes to shove on the world's linguistic stage.

Unfortunately, time rolls on. Juicy dollops of slang eventually lose their grunt and poke, drop off the twig of time and are consigned to the ashtray of history. While most good slang is welded to the tempo of the times, the language of our grandparents can still get us misty-eyed (even if some of it has all the menace of limp iceberg lettuce and is as cryptic as the poetry of Catullus).

'TEAM AUSTRALIA'

'HOOF ON THE TILL'

I'm not sure when I first understood the dry powder power of slang. I probably got thumped once or twice in the school playground on the way up, but I always thought I'd held my own in a stink if I could get a jab in with the tongue— before taking one and going down for the count.

Years later on the radio, as I waddled along the sporting beat, slang was a key to the insider's view of every competition. Sports buffs may not have a clue about what's happening on the park but well-chosen slang allows even the novices to appear plugged into the source. The colourful use of slang can have the audience leaning forward wondering, 'Did they really just say that? What on earth did they mean?'

For most of my working life, I've been lucky enough to work in the sporting coverage of radio and television. Shows like *This Sporting Life* (Triple J), *The Dream* (Channel Seven) and *Festival of the Boot* (Triple J and ABC NewsRadio) allowed my colleague, Rampaging Roy Slaven, and me to roam across the dial bending the language and creating our own slang. With several hours of airtime every week, it was possible to muscle new meanings onto simple words and phrases, allowing us to reset the linguistic landscape. There are rich pickings for language freaks in a world where too much sport is barely enough.

Understanding sporting slang makes you a member of the crew. This slang is crammed with a grim humour—Australians love to laugh at adversity. It's impossible to imagine the glorious uncertainty of horseracing without its dense and specific slang. Those on the losing end of the punt can be philosophical about having the shirt ripped from their back with the aid of it. Rich racing slang is a common language that's easy enough to rapidly unravel—take concepts like 'hoof on the till', 'be on me next time', 'smoking the pipe', 'smelling the field' and that fabulous image of a four-legged conveyance 'growing an extra leg in the wet'.

Rugby league coverage drips with slang. 'Going the grope', 'applying the squirrel grip' and 'reaching for the Christmas handshake' all refer to rugby league moves where the wedding tackle is the focus of the attack. This is considered very poor form, as the night tools are very important when the tune turns to horizontal folk dancing post hooter. After a vigorous Christmas handshake or a dismal performance, players are advised to 'go into the Room of Mirrors' and have 'a good hard look at themselves'. If a bustling ball-playing prop is tackled head high around 'the bonce', concussion often results, requiring a trip to 'the half dream room'. Once inside, coaches always stress the importance of being able to find 'the doorknob' that allows the mind to escape back to what is understood in rugby league circles as 'normality'.

'SQUIRREL GRIP'

'HULLO BOYS'

In 2000, I found myself in the odd position of being able to contribute a whole raft of slang to the world of words during the Sydney Olympics when covering the gymnastics competition. Terms like 'battered sav', 'hullo boys', 'crazy date', 'Dutch wink', 'spinning date', 'flat bag' and 'honey I'm home' were all moves tagged by Roy and me when fit young mat stars from all over the world went for gold. It took the viewers very little time to pick up the language we layered onto a sport that was tricky for the average punter to understand.

Slang does not always take off. Roy and I over the years have tried to popularise 'sloop pointing north', which ideally occurs during post-hooter horizontal folk dancing. We have failed. The boudoir is a very crowded linguistic market place in which we sadly could make little headway.

Slang has a great regional component. Because of the nation's size, South Australian slang is different from that of New South Wales, Western Australia's is vastly different from Victoria's, and so on. Different sports, different foods, different beer, different ambitions and different working circumstances all generate their own local linguistic responses. 'The Doctor' is a breeze that cools Perth on hot summer days.

'The coathanger' refers to the Sydney Harbour Bridge. Adelaide has 'fritz', a local luncheon meat, and 'the Kitchener bun'—two locally made linguistic gap fillers that baffle visitors, but have sustained generations of South Australian school kids. Melbourne has the 'G' where they play 'the Grannie' on that 'one day in September'. And so it goes.

In the modern social media world, state-based differences are being broken down rapidly. Everything and everyone is as close as the mobile phone in the hip pocket or handbag. But let's hope they don't all disappear as the slanguage of the future will be poorer without lively, local contributions.

Finally, an example of how quickly the whole caper moves on: the term, 'a Bradbury', indicating that an event was won because only one competitor was left standing at the finish line, was popularised after Steven Bradbury's amazing speed skating win in the 2002 Winter Olympics. Today, the term needs a lot of explanation.

H.G. NELSON

FAIR DINKUM

truthful; fair; possessing Australian honesty; are you telling me the truth?

Dinkum was British Midlands dialect for 'work' and 'fair dinkum' is probably derived from the idea of 'a fair day's dinkum'.

HAPPY LITTLE VEGEMITES

happy Australians, usually children

The Australian spreadable yeast extract market has several competitors. There's the English Marmite and the Australian so-sweet-it-may-as-well-be-American Promite. Both these blow-ins are overrated rubbish. It's completely un-Australian to be seen spreading these inferior products onto Mallee-grown wholegrain toast.

H.G.'s SPRAY

From an advertising jingle for Vegemite, *Happy Little Vegemites*, first aired in 1954.

CHEEKY
LITTLE
POSSUM

*an incorrigible
but humorous and
endearing person,
usually a child*

AS USEFUL
AS LIPS ON
A CHICKEN

useless

CROOK AS A CHOOK

very sick

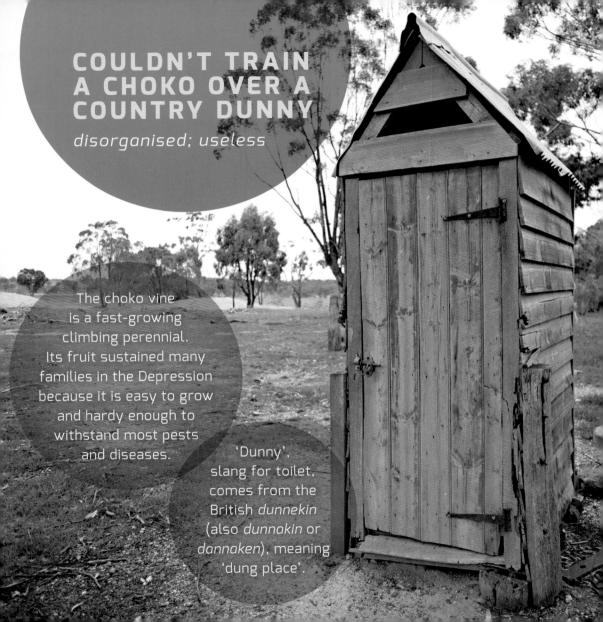

COULDN'T TRAIN A CHOKO OVER A COUNTRY DUNNY

disorganised; useless

The choko vine is a fast-growing climbing perennial. Its fruit sustained many families in the Depression because it is easy to grow and hardy enough to withstand most pests and diseases.

'Dunny', slang for toilet, comes from the British *dunnekin* (also *dunnakin* or *dannaken*), meaning 'dung place'.

**I HOPE YOUR CHOOKS
TURN INTO EMUS
AND KICK YOUR
DUNNY DOWN**

I wish you bad luck

A FEW SANDWICHES SHORT OF A PICNIC

stupid

COULDN'T ORGANISE A CHOOK RAFFLE AT A POULTRY FARM

disorganised; useless

MAD AS A CUT SNAKE

insane; very angry

MAKE A PROPER GALAH OF YOURSELF

make a fool of yourself

HE'S GOT A KANGAROO LOOSE IN THE TOP PADDOCK

crazy; stupid

GO TROPPO

go mad

Originating in the Second World War to describe the effect of prolonged engagements in the tropical jungles of South-East Asia on Australian servicemen.

AS SLOW AS A WET WEEK

*very slow;
boring*

H.G.'s
SPRAY

Given that the nation's in perpetual drought, this snap carries a boot load of irony. In a week that drags on forever, sometimes the most interesting thing to happen is the numbers spinning 'round on the petrol bowser.

Cooee was a locating cry in Dharug, the Aboriginal language in the Sydney area.

HIKERS TRACKS
TO LONG POINT ½ M.
TO RIVER 2½ M.

WITHIN COOEE

not too far away (distance, goal)

BOPEECHEE

ALICE SPRINGS 497M →
← 312 M. PORT PIRIE

WOOP
WOOP

*a very
remote place*

BACK OF BOURKE

a very remote place

H.G.'s SPRAY

There are remote patches of dirt across this sun-drenched land. But the nation's shrinking. Planes can go everywhere and motorbikes plug the gaps. Digital communication makes Bourke seem just over the horizon instead of in the middle of nowhere. Although Oodnadatta still requires two hands to find on the map.

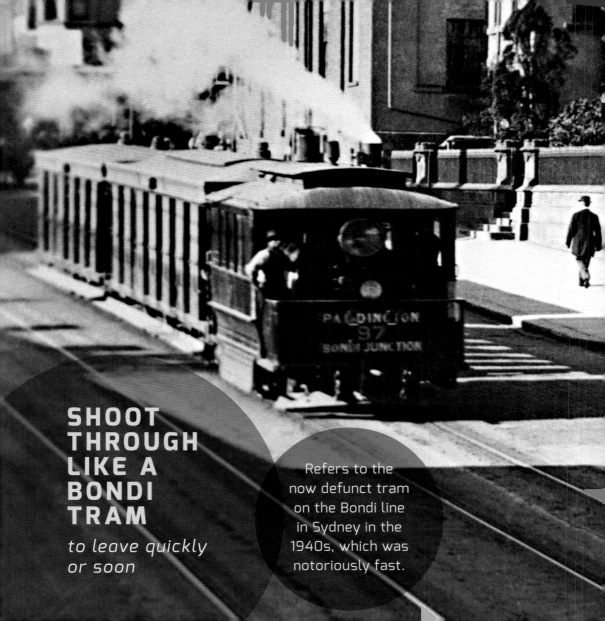

SHOOT THROUGH LIKE A BONDI TRAM

to leave quickly or soon

Refers to the now defunct tram on the Bondi line in Sydney in the 1940s, which was notoriously fast.

SEE YOU ROUND LIKE A RISSOLE

goodbye;
see you later

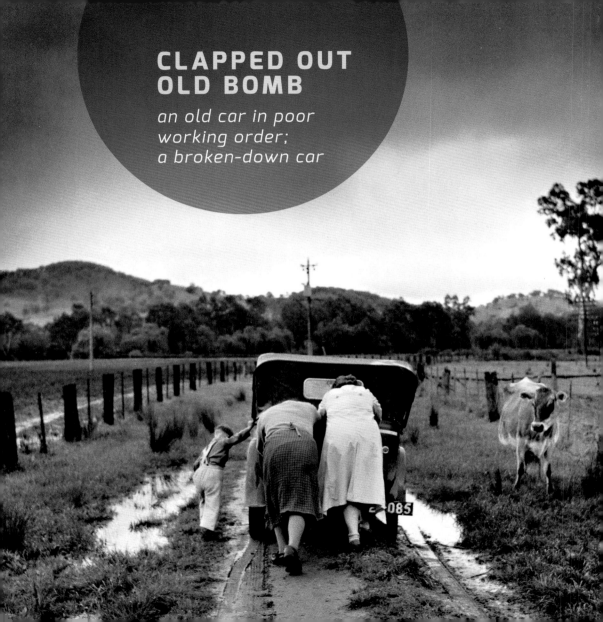

CLAPPED OUT OLD BOMB

an old car in poor working order; a broken-down car

CHUCK A U-EY

make a U-turn

SILLY DUFFER

*a person who has
made a silly mistake*

This phrase possibly
evolved from the
Scottish *duffar*,
meaning
'a stupid person'.

HE DOESN'T
KNOW IF
HE'S ARTHUR
OR MARTHA

he's confused

HE'S GOT TICKETS ON HIMSELF

he has an inflated ego

IN
LIKE
FLYNN

*a strong chance
of success*

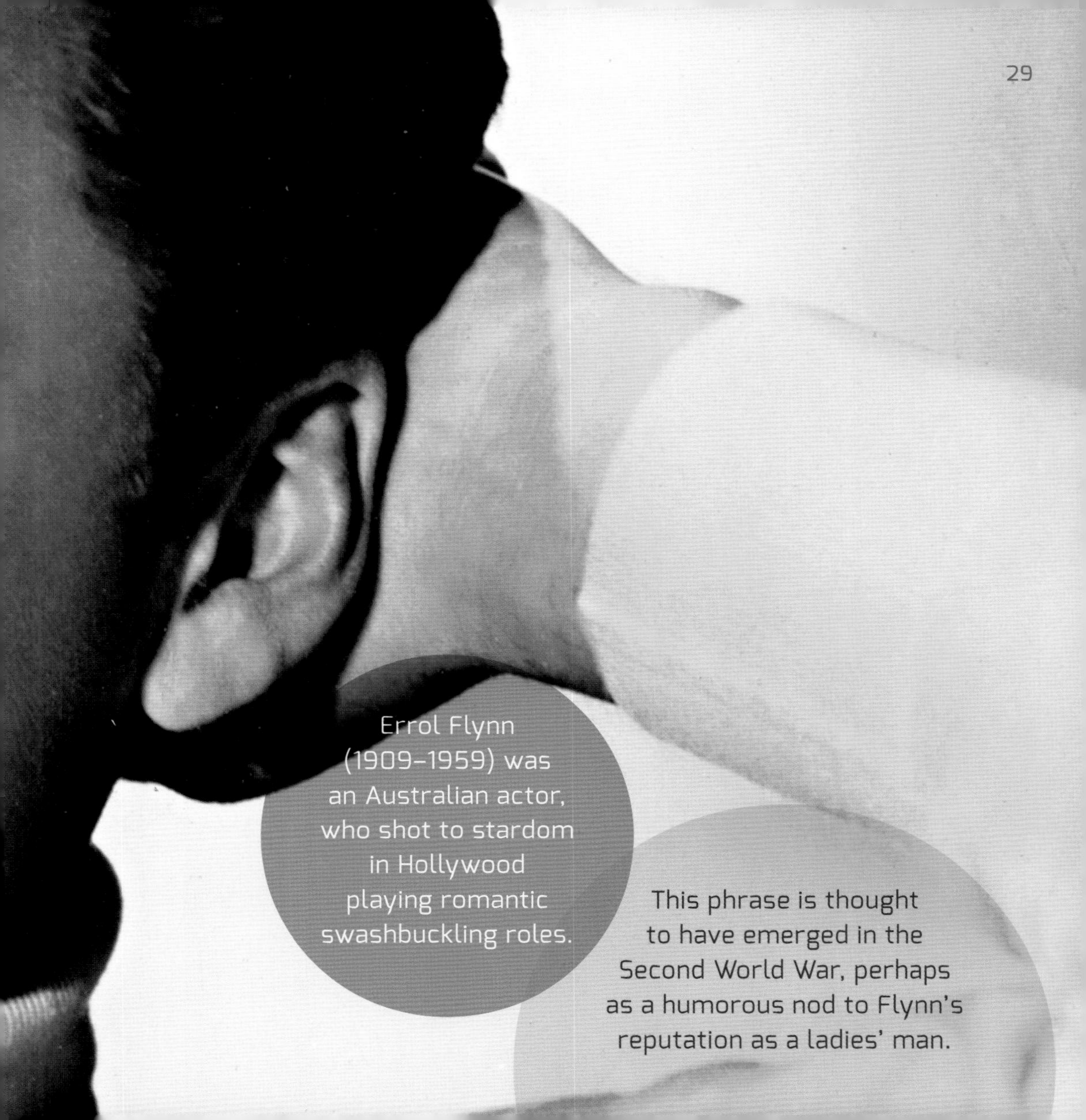

Errol Flynn
(1909–1959) was
an Australian actor,
who shot to stardom
in Hollywood
playing romantic
swashbuckling roles.

This phrase is thought
to have emerged in the
Second World War, perhaps
as a humorous nod to Flynn's
reputation as a ladies' man.

FLASH AS A
RAT WITH A
GOLD TOOTH

*dressed in an
ostentatious fashion;
untrustworthy*

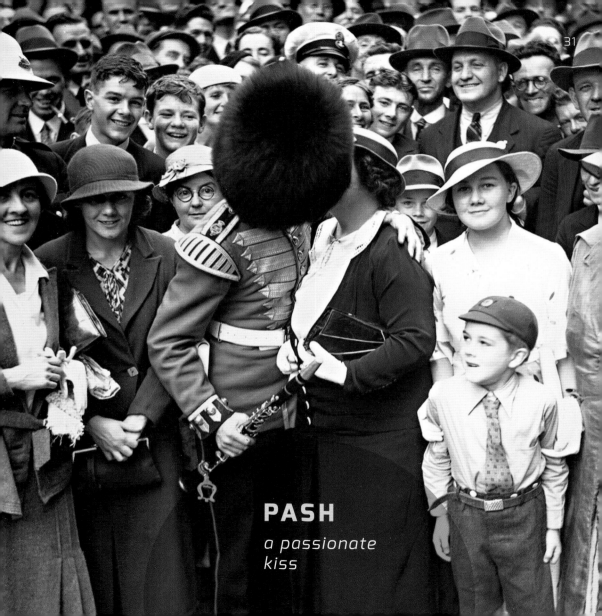

PASH

*a passionate
kiss*

TRUE BLUE

authentically Australian

H.G.'s SPRAY

No one went as far or as long as Slim Dusty. He made Australia his backyard. His classic, *A Pub with No Beer*, was once considered a starter for the national anthem. In the twenty-first century, when the world wants to be just like us, it's a crime not to be able to recite the first three verses of this rural hospitality epic.

G'DAY
hello

TUCKER
food

Used since the 1850s to refer to something that can be tucked away in your stomach.

SANGER
sandwich

FAIR GO
be fair; a fair opportunity

FAIR SHAKE OF THE SAUCE BOTTLE
be fair

SNAG

sausage

DRINKING WITH THE FLIES

drinking alone

BARBECUE STOPPER

an unexpected or shocking piece of information

LIKE FLIES 'ROUND A DUNNY DOOR

a throng of people attracted to something

WRAP YOUR LAUGHING GEAR 'ROUND THAT

eat that

FULL AS A GOOG

sated with food or alcohol

H.G.'s SPRAY

These two lads, Cyril and Cedric, have done a lot of work with the fork and the twenty-ounce glass. They've been at it for years. To construct this style of cantilevered verandah over the tool shed takes years of effort including the design phase, getting council permission and then all the heavy lifting. But the results are world class.

Possibly connected to the Scottish children's word, *goggie*, meaning 'egg'.

**A MAN'S
NOT A
CAMEL**

I need a drink

**DRIER
THAN A
DROVER'S
DOG**

very dry

Derived from *vin blanc*,
meaning 'white wine' in French,
pronounced as 'van blonk'
and then shortened to 'plonk'
by Australian soldiers
in the First World War.

PLONK

*wine;
cheap wine*

FLAT OUT LIKE A LIZARD DRINKING

very busy; exhausted

LOWER THAN A SNAKE'S BELLY

*despicable;
untrustworthy*

STREWTH!

that's shocking!;
wow!;
that was close!

H.G.'s SPRAY

Yesterday's acceptable swear word, overtaken, today, by 'Oh my God'. But bravely kept alive in the lingo of Alf from *Home and Away*, who appears to have a contract that requires him to blurt it once in every episode.

An abbreviated form of 'God's truth', originating in Britain.

LIKE A
STUNNED
MULLET

*shocked;
surprised*

STONE THE CROWS!

*wow!; I can't believe it!;
I'm unimpressed*

COP A LOAD OF THAT!

look at that!

BETTER THAN A POKE IN THE EYE WITH A BURNT STICK

it's not that bad

YOU'VE GOT BUCKLEY'S

you've got no chance of success

William Buckley (1780–1856) was an English convict who escaped and lived with the Wathaurung people of south-western Victoria for 32 years. Buckley's survival, thanks largely to the Indigenous peoples of the Bellarine Peninsula, was an improbable one. He eventually returned to European society.

NO WORRIES

that's okay; I don't mind

THINGS ARE CROOK IN TALLAROOK

things are not going well

DON'T COME THE RAW PRAWN WITH ME!

don't cheat or lie to me

CHUCK A SICKIE

take a day off work as sick leave even if not sick

FURPHY

misleading or false, but commonly believed, story

During the First World War, John Furphy's water carts were the 'water coolers' of the day— places where people would congregate and gossip.

IT'S SO WINDY IT COULD BLOW A DOG OFF A CHAIN

it's very windy

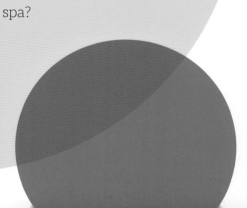

H.G.'s
SPRAY

With climate on the move, this graphic expression is one that may get a second wind and become hip again. But our relationship with the four-legged community has changed so much that not many Spots are chained up these days. It's so windy it could blow Buster out of his day spa?

BUDGIE SMUGGLERS

men's revealing swimming costume

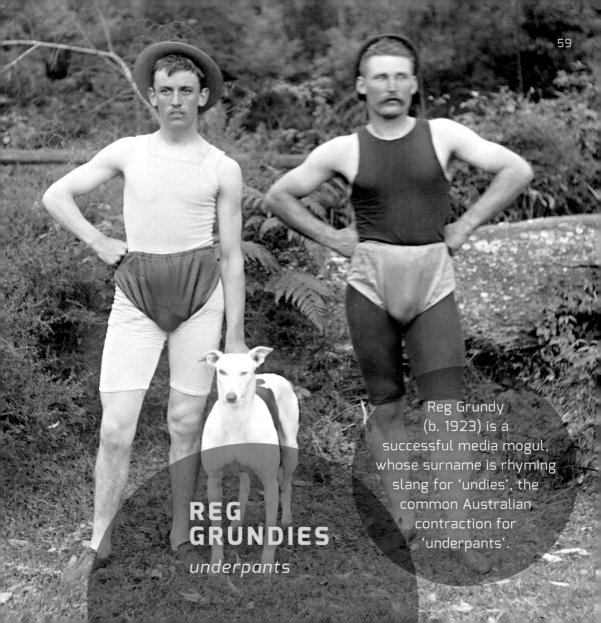

REG GRUNDIES

underpants

Reg Grundy (b. 1923) is a successful media mogul, whose surname is rhyming slang for 'undies', the common Australian contraction for 'underpants'.

DAG

*an unfashionable
but lovable
person*

A bludgeoner was
a person who used a
bludgeon as a weapon.
This evolved to mean
'a prostitute's pimp',
one living off the
earnings of another.

BLUDGER

*a person
who doesn't
contribute
his or her
fair share*

BOGAN
*an uncultured
person lacking
class; a boor*

DINKY-DI

*authentically
Australian*

WOWSER

*a person who is easily
morally outraged;
a prude; a killjoy*

Possibly related to the British
verb *wow*, meaning 'to complain'
or perhaps an acronym standing
for We Only Want Social Evils
Righted. John Norton, editor
of *Truth* magazine, claimed
to have coined it in 1899.

PANIC
MERCHANT

*a person who
panics easily*

BOOFHEAD

an idiot

DROPKICK

an idiot

DRONGO

an idiot

Probably after an Australian horse of the same name, which ran 37 races in the early 1920s without a win.

OCKER

stereotypically unsophisticated Australian

**I WOULDN'T
BE DEAD
FOR QUIDS**

I'm enjoying life!

GOING OFF LIKE A FROG IN A SOCK

very successful (of an event);
losing your temper;
doing something very
energetically

RUNNING AROUND LIKE A CHOOK WITH ITS HEAD CUT OFF

panicking; overreacting

**FLAT
CHAT**
at full speed

OFF LIKE A BUCKET OF PRAWNS IN THE SUN

to leave quickly or soon

H.G.'s SPRAY

Mercifully refrigeration has been invented so this stylish slang response to any stink has gone the way of the Muttaburrasaurus. Of course one of the great Australian stories is the tale of keeping things cool. The Coolgardie safe and the Esky were great early attempts, but the Kelvinator brought it home. Not sure anyone could find buckets of prawns to go off in the sun round Nowra in this day and age.

CHUCK A
WOBBLY

*throw a tantrum;
lose your temper*

HE COULD TALK UNDER WET CEMENT

he's extremely talkative

NOT ENOUGH
BRAINS TO
GIVE HIMSELF
A HEADACHE

stupid

BUGGER THAT FOR A JOKE

I can't accept that!

HARD YAKKA

hard work, usually physical labour

Originally a Yagara word, from the Brisbane region, but used in Australian English since the 1880s.

GAME AS NED

*very brave
(also, foolishly so)*

**H.G.'s
SPRAY**

Ned is one of this nation's greatest inventors. He was the man who cut a hole in the front of a rubbish bin and put it on his head when he saw the cops coming. 'Such is life' was one of his. It's a hell of a phrase to go out on.

Edward 'Ned' Kelly (1854–1880) was an Australian bushranger who committed daring and brazen crimes across Victoria, before being caught, convicted and hanged at Old Melbourne Gaol.

**SHE'LL
BE RIGHT**

things will be okay

SHE'S APPLES

everything's fine

Derived from
the rhyming slang
phrase for nice,
'apple and spice'.

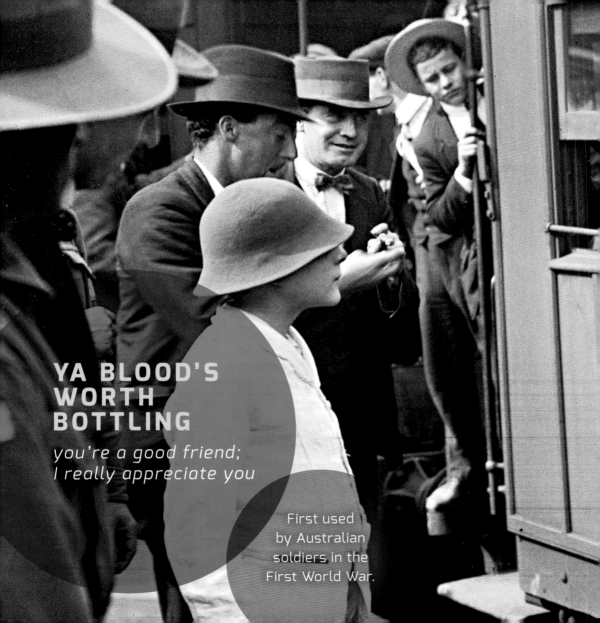

YA BLOOD'S WORTH BOTTLING

*you're a good friend;
I really appreciate you*

First used
by Australian
soldiers in the
First World War.

**FACE LIKE A
DROPPED PIE**

very ugly

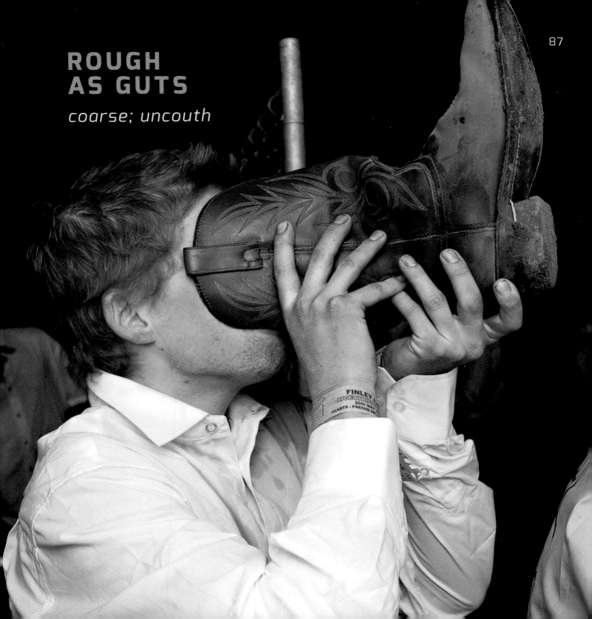

ROUGH
AS GUTS

coarse; uncouth

HEAD LIKE A BEATEN FAVOURITE

very ugly

H.G.'s
SPRAY

Appearances have always been
a rich source of slang. 'Face like a
Mallee root' and 'face like a dropped pie'
plus this gem remind us how creative
the slang generated by our looks can be.
Stating the bruised and bleeding obvious,
the art of the sweet science is not to
get punched continuously in the
head, the process that results in
a 'head like a beaten favourite'.

Originally from the Hindi *chāp*, meaning 'a stamp or brand', the phrase 'first chop' was used in the British Raj to mean 'highest quality'.

NOT MUCH CHOP

poor quality

'AVE A GO,
YA MUG!

*try harder,
you useless
individual!*

BARRACK FOR

*support a sporting
team or player*

Originally,
a Northern Irish
word meaning
'to brag'.

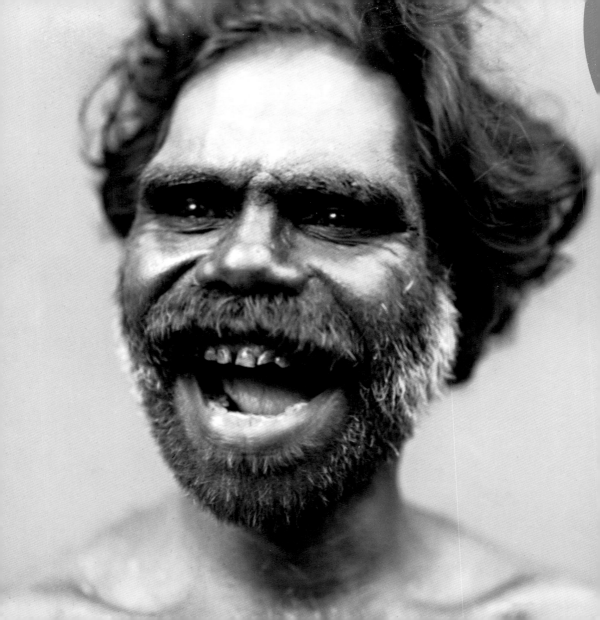

HAPPY AS LARRY

extremely happy or content

H.G.'s SPRAY

Not sure who the original
Larry was. Or how happy he was.
But from the photographic evidence
he was a riot in the right context.
Must've been great to have over for a
birthday or a family Christmas. The stories!
Sadly, Larry is no longer a contemporary
Australian first name. Dane and Bryce,
that's more like it. But 'happy as Dane'
and 'happy as Bryce' just don't
have the same authority.

BUNG

not working; injured

Originally a Yagara word, from the Brisbane area, meaning 'dead'.

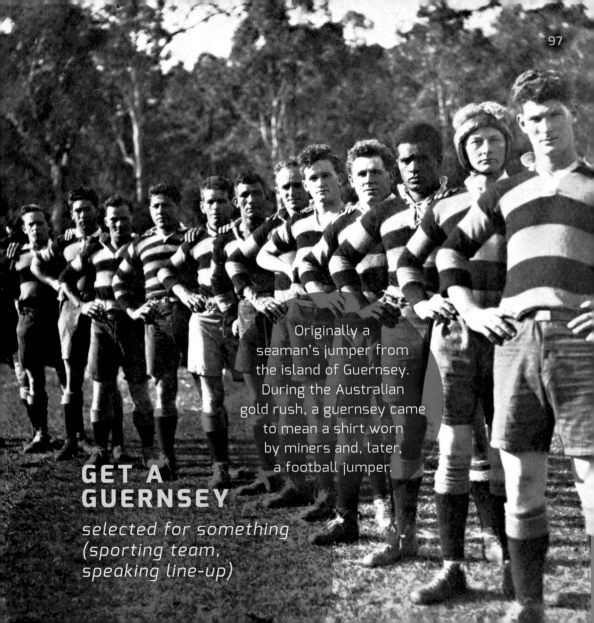

Originally a seaman's jumper from the island of Guernsey. During the Australian gold rush, a guernsey came to mean a shirt worn by miners and, later, a football jumper.

GET A GUERNSEY

selected for something (sporting team, speaking line-up)

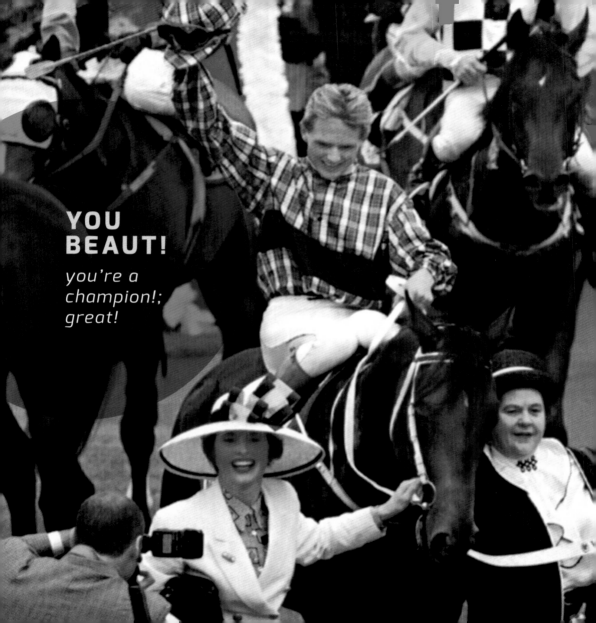

YOU
BEAUT!

you're a champion!; great!

GIVE IT A BURL, SHIRL

give something a try

A *burl* is a 'spin' or 'whirl' in Scottish English. This phrase is a variation of the British, 'give it a whirl'.

FAIR CRACK OF THE WHIP!

you're not being fair!

FIT AS A MALLEE BULL

very strong and healthy

Mallee is probably an Aboriginal word from the area of western Victoria now known by that name.

EVERY MAN
AND HIS DOG

everybody

CHOCKERS
full; overcrowded

Chock-a-block was a nautical phrase, probably used from the nineteenth century onwards, describing a block and tackle hoisted as high as possible.

LIST OF ILLUSTRATIONS

Many of these illustrations are details. For full images, see the National Library of Australia's catalogue at **nla.gov.au.**

PAGE 16
Bill Bachman
Floodway Sign beside a Desert Road in Channel Country near Boulia, Queensland 1990
colour photograph; 24.7 x 51.1 cm
nla.gov.au/nla.cat-vn5746489

PAGE 18
Steam Tram on the Paddington and Bondi Route in Elizabeth Street near the Supreme Court, Sydney c. 1900
b&w photograph; 21.5 x 15.7 cm
nla.gov.au/nla.cat-vn4778608

PAGE 19
Charles Louis Gabriel (1857–1927)
Passenger Looking out through the Railway Carriage Window, Gundagai Station, Gundagai, New South Wales between 1887 and 1927
b&w glass negative; 10.1 x 12.6 cm
nla.gov.au/nla.cat-vn2267320

PAGES 20–21
Joyce Evans
Desert Car on Gunbarrel Highway, Northern Territory 1991
colour photograph; 21 x 50.6 cm
nla.gov.au/nla.cat-vn6260885

PAGE 22
Jeff Carter (1928–2010)
Tobacco Road c. 1955
b&w photograph; 30.8 x 26.8 cm
nla.gov.au/nla.cat-vn2374843
© Jeff Carter Archive

PAGE 23
Francis Birtles' Dog Dinkum behind the Wheel of a Car c. 1924
b&w photograph; 7.2 x 10 cm
nla.gov.au/nla.cat-vn5399781

PAGES 24–25
Three Children on a Crocodile 1927
colour lantern slide; 8.2 x 8.2 cm
nla.gov.au/nla.cat-vn2115802

PAGE 26
Bruce Howard (b. 1936)
Variation on a Theme at the Fancy Dress Ball at the Pub in Tennant Creek, Northern Territory 1972
b&w photograph; 30.2 x 22.9 cm
nla.gov.au/nla.cat-vn4361381

PAGE 27
Male Performer in Tuxedo Flanked by Two Female Performers in Ruffled Dresses and with Bows in Their Hair, for J.C. Williamson Production 1910s
b&w photograph; 19.9 x 10.8 cm
nla.gov.au/nla.cat-vn3601085

PAGES 28–29
Portrait of Errol Flynn 1930s
b&w photograph; 25.3 x 18.3 cm
nla.gov.au/nla.cat-vn3673140

PAGE 30
Don Nicol in Costume Holding Straw Hat and Cane between 1936 and 1947
b&w photograph; 24.4 x 19.6 cm
nla.gov.au/nla.cat-vn3600765

PAGE 31
S.J. Hood
A Member of the Band of His Majesty's Grenadier Guards Kissing a Person in Crowd in Martin Place, Sydney, after a Ceremony at the Cenotaph 1934
b&w photograph; 15 x 20 cm
nla.gov.au/nla.cat-vn3508437

PAGE 32
Bruce Howard (b. 1936)
Slim Dusty at the Pub with No Beer, the Palace Hotel, Southern Cross, Western Australia c. 1972
b&w photograph; 20 x 30.1 cm
nla.gov.au/nla.cat-vn4361515

PAGE 34-35
William Yang (b. 1943)
Michael Xu at the Party after His Citizenship Ceremony 1997
b&w photograph; 29.6 x 40.3 cm
nla.gov.au/nla.cat-vn240397

PAGE 36
Favourite Australian Dishes (Canberra: Commonwealth Office of Education, c. 1949)
colour poster; 57 x 45 cm
nla.gov.au/nla.cat-vn5717556

PAGE 37 (left)
Raymond De Berquelle (b. 1933)
Australian Barbeque of Lamb Chops, Sausages and Onion Rings at Strathfield, New South Wales 1978
colour photograph; 24.9 x 33.2 cm
nla.gov.au/nla.cat-vn4386064

PAGE 37 (right)
Bruce Howard (b. 1936)
Drinking on the Water's Edge, Fanny Bay, Darwin, Northern Territory c. 1971
b&w photograph; 21.5 x 15.9 cm
nla.gov.au/nla.cat-vn4361471

PAGES 38–39
Jeff Carter (1928–2010)
Four Children Eating Freshly Shucked Oysters from the Shell, New South Wales c. 1960
b&w photograph; 33 x 48.2 cm
nla.gov.au/nla.cat-vn3991039
© Jeff Carter Archive

PAGE 40
Graham S. Burstow
The Finalists 1985
b&w photograph; 32.5 x 43 cm
nla.gov.au/nla.cat-vn3279498

PAGE 65
Bob Nicol
A Welcome Drink at the Mount Carbine Hotel for Cattlemen and Drivers of Cattle Transports 1971
b&w photograph; 9 x 9 cm
nla.gov.au/nla.cat-vn4589902
Australian News and Information Bureau

PAGES 66–67
Rennie Ellis (1940–2003)
Robert DiPierdomenico 'Dipper', MCG 1986
colour photograph; 29.3 x 44 cm
nla.gov.au/nla.cat-vn4103266

PAGE 68
David Moore (1927–2003)
Outback Children, South Australia 1963
b&w photograph; 38 x 27 cm
nla.gov.au/nla.cat-vn2258302

PAGE 69
Tea under the Mulberry Tree
page 29 in *The Australian Women's Weekly*,
7 January 1959
nla.gov.au/nla.news-page4912147

PAGES 70–71
Bill Bachman
Noel Fullerton Riding Camel Malachi down a Sand Dune, Rainbow Valley, Northern Territory c. 1982 (2012 printing)
colour photograph; 51.1 x 33.6 cm
nla.gov.au/nla.cat-vn5746467

PAGE 72
Jeff Carter (1928–2010)
Prawn Fisherman with Baskets of Prawns at Greenwell Point near Nowra, New South Wales c. 1955
b&w photograph; 48.2 x 33 cm
nla.gov.au/nla.cat-vn3991127
© Jeff Carter Archive

PAGE 74
Impatiently Waiting for His Dinner 1939
b&w photograph; 18.9 x 14.1 cm
nla.gov.au/nla.cat-vn3511892

PAGE 75
Mr J. Harrington Talking with an Unidentified Man, New South Wales 1920s
b&w glass negative; 8.3 x 10.8 cm
nla.gov.au/nla.cat-vn6251139
Courtesy Fairfax Syndication
www.fairfaxsyndication.com

PAGE 76
Herbert H. Fishwick (1882–1957)
Man Sitting on the Back of an Ostrich, Temora, New South Wales 1912
b&w glass negative; 12 x 16.3 cm
nla.gov.au/nla.cat-vn6334568
Courtesy Fairfax Syndication
www.fairfaxsyndication.com

PAGE 77
Charles Troedel & Co.
Poor Dolly
(Melbourne: Australasian Sketcher, 1887)
colour lithograph; 55.9 x 40.7 cm
nla.gov.au/nla.cat-vn1844636

PAGES 78–79
Hot Work by Australian Gunners
between 1939 and 1945
colour postcard; 8.9 x 13.8 cm
nla.gov.au/nla.cat-vn3578962

PAGE 80
Bruce Howard (b. 1936)
Ned Kelly and a Medieval Lady at the Fancy Dress Ball at the Pub in Tennant Creek, Northern Territory 1972
b&w photograph; 25.3 x 20.4 cm
nla.gov.au/nla.cat-vn4361475

PAGE 82
Rennie Ellis (1940–2003)
My Son Josh Learns to Swim 1972
b&w photograph; 30.4 x 43.7 cm
nla.gov.au/nla.cat-vn4082332

PAGE 83
Young Girl Holding a Large Apple beside Her Head, New South Wales 1930s
b&w glass negative; 12 x 16.3 cm
nla.gov.au/nla.cat-vn6342863
Courtesy Fairfax Syndication
www.fairfaxsyndication.com

PAGES 84–85
Herbert H. Fishwick (1882–1957)
New Recruit Leaning out of a Train Window to Shake Hands with a Wounded Soldier, New South Wales c. 1915
b&w glass negative; 12 x 16.3 cm
nla.gov.au/nla.cat-vn6329187
Courtesy Fairfax Syndication
www.fairfaxsyndication.com

PAGE 86
Herbert H. Fishwick (1882–1957)
Study of a Bull Dog, New South Wales 1930s
b&w glass negative; 12 x 16.3 cm
nla.gov.au/nla.cat-vn6341783
Courtesy Fairfax Syndication
www.fairfaxsyndication.com

PAGE 87
Michael Coyne (b. 1945)
Bachelor and Spinster Ball, Drinking from Boot, Finley, New South Wales 2006
colour photograph; 19.6 cm x 25.6 cm
nla.gov.au/nla.cat-vn3800775

PAGE 88
Jack Hassen and Joe Brown during a Boxing Match at West Melbourne Stadium, Melbourne 1950
b&w photograph; 19.4 x 24 cm
nla.gov.au/nla.cat-vn3646896

PAGE 90
Jeff Carter (1928–2010)
Tomorrow's Champion Wood Cutter, Berry, New South Wales 2003
b&w photograph; 42 x 26 cm
nla.gov.au/nla.cat-vn4231273
© Jeff Carter Archive

LEARN MORE

Readers can learn more
Australian slang, and find out
about the etymology of
slang words and phrases,
using the following excellent
online resources:

Macquarie Dictionary,
www.macquariedictionary.com.au
'Meanings and Origins of Australian Words and Idioms',
Australian National Dictionary Centre,
Australian National University,
andc.anu.edu.au/australian-words/meanings-origins

FAIR DINKUM!
AUSSIE SLANG

Get a guernsey
    selected for something (sporting team, speaking line-up)

Give it a burl, Shirl
    give something a try

Go troppo
    go mad

Going off like a frog in a sock
    very successful (of an event); losing your temper; doing something very energetically

Happy as Larry
    extremely happy or content

Happy little Vegemites
    happy Australians, usually children

Hard yakka
    hard work, usually physical labour

He could talk under wet cement
    he's extremely talkative

He doesn't know if he's Arthur or Martha
    he's confused

Head like a beaten favourite
    very ugly

He's got a kangaroo loose in the top paddock
    crazy; stupid

He's got tickets on himself
    he has an inflated ego

I hope your chooks turn into emus and kick your dunny down
    I wish you bad luck

I wouldn't be dead for quids
    I'm enjoying life!

In like Flynn
    a strong chance of success

It's so windy it could blow a dog off a chain
    it's very windy

Like a stunned mullet
    shocked; surprised

Like flies 'round a dunny door
    a throng of people attracted to something

Lower than a snake's belly
    despicable; untrustworthy

Mad as a cut snake
    insane; very angry

Make a proper galah of yourself
    make a fool of yourself

No worries
    that's okay; I don't mind

Not enough brains to give himself a headache
    stupid

Not much chop
    poor quality

Ocker
    stereotypically unsophisticated Australian

Off like a bucket of prawns in the sun
    to leave quickly or soon